THE ENVIRONMENT AND YOU

Written by MATTHEW J. BRENNAN

Illustrated by ANTHONY TALLARICO

(Abridged)

GROSSET & DUNLAP • Publishers • NEW YORK

Introduction

You are at the start of an exciting adventure —an adventure in discovery, understanding and action. And fortunately you have a highly skilled guide to lead you. Dr. Matthew J. Brennan has for many years devoted himself to learning and teaching environmental studies. He knows his way, and knows how to help others find theirs.

"But," you may ask, "why are we setting out on an *environmental* exploration rather than on some other?"

The reason is that you and your environment —your classroom, your school, your home, your street, your neighborhood and what lies beyond it—are inescapably linked together. Furthermore, you as an individual depend for your existence and indeed for your survival on the health of each of the many parts that constitute the total environment. Unfortunately, as you have no doubt observed, many of these component parts are today in a dangerously unhealthy state.

When people first became concerned with the condition of our environment, they were called Conservationists. These early crusaders, realizing that we were violating the rules of nature, concentrated their attention on earth's four great renewable resources—soil, water, forests and wildlife.

Gradually it became clear that this view was far too limited. Many of us no longer live in a rural region where there are plenty of trees and meadows, plenty of streams, fish, and game. Most of us now live in suburbs or in cities. We struggle with problems of overcrowding, traffic tie-ups, of miserable and inadequate housing with lack of open spaces for relaxing and playing. You can probably name other conditions in your environment which need a change for the better.

If you want to help to produce such change you will need to become an Environmentalist, a person determined to save and improve the environment by working *with* nature's principles rather than *against* them. An Environmentalist needs an understanding of the basic laws of Ecology, the science that deals with the interrelationship of living things with each other and with their environment.

The term ecology stems from the Greek *oikos* meaning home and *logy* meaning science. Thus ecology is really a study of sound housekeeping of our planetary home. This home or habitat includes slums as well as countryside; our problems encompass poverty as well as dirty air or filthy water; our tasks include the rebuilding of our cities as well as the reusing of our wastes.

Under Dr. Brennan's guidance you will learn in detail about the environmental problems that face us all, and some of the steps that need to be taken to solve them. In addition, you will discover what *you* can do to help in restoring our planet as a life-supporting, life-enriching home for us, our fellow creatures and those who come after us.

MARTHA MUNZER

Martha Munzer is an Associate of the Wave Hill Center for Environmental Studies in New York City and the author of numerous books, both for children and adults, on the subject of conservation and environmental quality.

ISBN: 0-448-04060-3 (Trade Edition)
ISBN: 0-448-03865-X (Library Edition)
ISBN: 0-448-05071-4 (Wonder Book Edition)

Abridged Grosset & Dunlap edition, 1973
Copyright © 1972 J. G. Ferguson Publishing Company
Printed in the United States of America
1974 PRINTING

Contents

The Meaning of Environment

Close your eyes and think of a living room. Everyone knows what a living room is like. A living room has a sofa, some chairs, some tables, perhaps a television set, a rug on the floor, and pictures on the wall. But is your living room — the one you thought of when you closed your eyes — the same as your friend's? Of course not. Even though many living rooms contain the same types of items, they all look different. The furniture is different, the pictures are different, the arrangement is different. Some living rooms have pianos or hi-fi sets; some do not.

What does this have to do with our environment? A living room is a part of our environment — it is a place in which we live. We affect it, we control its temperature. We are affected by it if it is too hot, too cold, too noisy, or has a bad odor. People have always been concerned with the appearance and quality of their living rooms. Recently, they have also become concerned with the appearance and quality of their total environment.

In this book, we will learn about our total environment and the concerns which man has for its quality, and what you can do to help to restore our environment to a condition of beauty and bounty.

What is our environment? Our environment is the whole earth and everything in it and on it. It is the world around us. It includes not only the environment around us but the environment within us — a total environment. Our environment also includes all of the conditions which have an effect on our lives.

In the relatively short period that man has lived on the earth, he has caused great changes in the environment in his effort to supply his needs and the luxuries of living. Man has cultivated some of the wild plants, and

Our total environment is the planet earth. Our actions affect all living and nonliving matter on it.

tamed some of the wild animals for food, clothing, and pets. He has cleared the vast forests which once covered much of the earth to make room for his cities and to supply his needs for building materials. He has searched the earth for minerals and oil and refined them for his use as fuel, materials for housing and industry, and tools and machines for his advancing technology.

Man has built a great civilization using the resources of the environment, but has given little thought to the consequences of the changes he was making. Now, at last, concern for the effects of man's activities on the quality of the environment and life is becoming widespread.

Why is man becoming concerned about

Why the new concern for the quality of the environment? the quality of the environment? Why has he not been concerned before? Man has always considered his resources to be without limit, especially in the United States, a nation with a wealth of resources of all kinds.

At one time, the forests of America were thought to be inexhaustible. The soil was rich, producing crops in enor-

Some of the first environmentalists in America were Indians. They lived in harmony with the land they settled, and did not poison the water, exhaust the soil, or cause air pollution.

mous quantity. So great was the quantity of food production that great surpluses were stored and fed to animals to produce meat, dairy products, eggs, and the protein-rich foods our affluent nation demanded. Vast quantities of wildlife abounded. Great tracts of wilderness were available for man's recreation. There was so much land that man had no thought of any shortage. Except for a few cities, the air over the nation was clear and fresh, the water in the rivers and lakes was pure.

What happened, then, to change the beauty and bounty of this rich land? How could we ever reach a point in our history when men would compete for food, for room in which to live and play, for air fit to breathe, and water fit to drink? Our lights dim as electric power sources prove inadequate to supply our ever-increasing needs. Even in this country some people go hungry, and millions of people on earth starve to death every year. Some scientists now question man's ability to survive in this new environment.

To make it easier for us to investigate the crisis in the environment, we can separate the problems into four major groups — the "P" problems of the environment. The "P" problems are pollution, poisons, poverty of the environment, and population.

Herds of buffalo and bison once roamed the Western plains in such quantity it was possible to shoot great numbers of them from trains for "sport." So many were killed the species almost became extinct.

Pollution

Let us think of our living room again.

What is pollution? Imagine your living room with a pile of garbage in it, or so noisy you can't even relax or think, or filled with smoke, or even too hot to stay in. There are many ways a living room — or any environment — can be polluted: by wastes, noise, heat, smoke or chemical fumes, or anything that doesn't fit in with *your* concept of a living room. Pollution can be a very personal thing. What constitutes noise pollution in the adults' living room may be "groovy" music in the living room of the young.

Pollution also depends on location. A pile of abandoned cars in a junk yard may not be considered pollution, but the same pile of junked cars in a grassy field along a highway may well be con-

An abandoned car shouldn't be left to rust at the side of a pretty road. It is one form of pollution.

sidered pollution. Pollution is a condition in which something is found in the environment which doesn't belong there, or which causes unpleasant or ugly consequences there. In short, an environment is polluted if it is filled with objects or events (happenings) which contaminate it.

There are many kinds of pollution, but

What kinds of pollution exist? they can be grouped into several major headings: air pollution, water pollution, land pollution, noise pollution, and radiation pollution. Let us consider briefly each of these kinds of pollution and its possible effects on the environment and life on earth.

"Smog levels are high today," the radio

What is air pollution? or TV weather reporter says. And millions of Americans head through the smog to their place of work. Smog makes people uncomfortable. It irritates the eyes, ears, nose, and throat. It affects the functions of

The combination of smoke and fog that we call smog is not just an annoyance. Smog produces dangerous flying and driving conditions, and scientists suspect it is the cause of some serious diseases.

the lungs to the extent that some people become ill. Smog reduces visibility and increases the dangers of flying and driving. Some scientists believe that smog may cause cancer of the lungs and respiratory system.

What is smog, and where does it come from? Smog is produced by the action of sunlight (photo-chemical action) on two of the principal waste products of the automobile engine (the internal combustion engine), hydrocarbons and nitrogen oxides. It is estimated by scientists that over 25 million

tons of hydrocarbons and nearly 20 million tons of nitrogen oxides go into the air over the United States every year, and about half of these wastes come from motor vehicle use.

Another automobile engine exhaust waste product, perhaps even more dangerous than smog, is the colorless, odorless, tasteless, but deadly carbon monoxide (CO). It is produced by the incomplete burning of gasoline. Man has known about the lethal nature of carbon monoxide since the invention of the gasoline engine and has learned

Motor vehicles release a number of dangerous exhaust emissions, including deadly carbon monoxide. Inhalation of carbon monoxide can cause headaches, loss of vision and muscle coordination, and even fainting.

Industrial air pollution is often caused by the burning of coal and oil containing large amounts of sulphur.

to avoid it. We have all been taught to be sure the garage doors are open before we start our car's engine.

Today we all breathe in some carbon monoxide most of the time, nearly all of the time if we live in a city, for nearly 100 million tons go into the air over the United States each year. Carbon monoxide is a dangerous poison. It is particularly dangerous because while we cannot see, smell, or taste it, it has a detrimental effect on the body. Carbon monoxide combines chemically with the hemoglobin in red blood cells much more easily and rapidly than oxygen. When it is present in the air we breathe, the blood cells carry carbon monoxide, and do not pick up and carry the oxygen which is vital to our life processes. Recent studies have shown that the results of inhaling carbon monoxide can be headaches, loss of energy, vision, and muscular coordination. Heart disease patients seem to be especially susceptible to carbon monoxide poisoning and its effects.

In addition to the three kinds of chemicals listed above, engine exhausts also emit particulates (tiny bits of matter) such as lead, asbestos, and smoke. Lead, almost 200 million tons annually, is used in gasolines to increase power and reduce engine knock. Many oil companies now realize the danger of lead particulates, and are producing a non-leaded gasoline.

While the automobiles, buses, and trucks on the highways are the principal producers of air pollutants, they are not wholly responsible. Some of the most common contributors to air pollution are the sulphur oxides, most of which are produced by burning coal and oil which contain large amounts of sulphur. These waste chemicals are especially irritating, since they produce sulphuric acid when they come in contact with moist membranes, such as those within the eye, nose, throat, or lungs.

Who causes air pollution?

Burning of garbage and waste paper in incinerators and open dumps is another major contributor to the air pollution problem. In addition to the smoke, soot, and ash produced by burning materials, potentially dangerous chemicals can be released from burning plastics or aerosol containers used for paints, hair sprays, antiperspirants, air fresheners, and dry cleaning aids.

Most such burning has been controlled in an effort to reduce air pollution. But the problems are complex and solutions are difficult. If we stop burning wastes, they accumulate as solids. If we eliminate hydrocarbons, the nitrogen oxides in engine exhausts become water pollutants, as we shall see in the next section.

"Just dump it in the lake, stream, or ocean. Nature will take care of it." That is the assumption under which man has disposed of the wastes of his body, his home, his farms, his factories, and his cities since the beginning of his existence. In most places, it is still the method of waste disposal. Man has not advanced much in his desire or his actions to reduce the pollution of the earth's waters during his history. In the middle ages, men threw their garbage and body wastes out the door. The rain then carried them down to the river, lake, or sea. Today, many centuries later, man has advanced only to the point where he now carries the wastes to the river, lake, or sea through a pipe.

What is water pollution?

But now, at last, man is concerned about the problem. Let us examine the problems man now faces in his efforts to restore the quality of his water environment. What are the pollutants and who are the polluters?

If enough untreated sewage wastes are pumped into this lake, it will become unfit for marine life and be destroyed as a source of fresh water.

11

American homes have been the source of a number of pollutants, but two have contributed significantly to the water pollution problem which faces the nation — sewage and household detergents. Even in our modern nation, there are many communities with no sewage treatment facilities at all. Sewage is simply piped into the neighborhood water supply. In the early years of our nation, when the population was small, the natural action of bacteria and air changed the wastes into soluble nitrates and phosphates, which served as a mineral source for plants and animals living in the water. But as the population increased, the natural processes could no longer keep the waters clean for use by other living things or communities.

How is water polluted in the home?

Even communities with the most modern sewage treatment plants contribute to the water pollution problem. The problem is that treatment procedures were designed to assist in the natural processes of waste recycling by turning solid wastes into supposedly harmless phosphates and nitrates — nature's fertilizers. Indeed, they are nature's fertilizers. They have been absorbed by algae and other green plants that live in water. With the help of these fertilizers, these plants have grown into masses of vegetation which are choking our waterways and, in places like Lake Erie, polluting the waters and shores with their decaying masses. In the process of decay, these masses of plant materials use up all the oxygen in the water, making it an unfit environment for fish.

We will see later that animal wastes, fertilizers, and auto exhausts add to the fertilizing process which is polluting the waters of the earth. Even the oceans do not escape. Many of the nation's largest coastal cities either pipe their sewage directly into the ocean or carry the sewage effluent from their treatment plants on barges out into the ocean for dumping. Large areas of the Atlantic Ocean off New York City have been made unfit for marine life by these wastes.

How do detergents pollute the water?

Man's use of detergents and other cleaning materials is the other large source of water pollution. It also gives us one of the best examples of man's failure to consider the possible consequences of changes he makes in the environment. How did it all start? Man first used soap to wash his clothes. But soap did not work well in hard water, that is, water with a high mineral content. Clothes washed in hard water did not get really clean. The soapy water left a bathtub ring around the tub after the bath.

So, the soap manufacturers produced a new product, a detergent which made white clothes "whiter than white." Americans had the whitest washes in the world. But what happened when the detergents washed into the nation's waterways? The bacteria had broken down the soaps (chiefly made from tallow) just as they broke down sewage. The detergents, however, presented a new problem. They were not affected by bacterial action in the waters. They lasted forever! Every time the detergent-filled waters were agitated by sewage treatment or shaken up as they floated down streams, a new mass of suds developed. In many areas, lakes and streams were covered by foaming suds.

Again, the soap manufacturers went to work on a new detergent which could be broken down by bacterial action. The result was the phosphate detergent, which continued the white washes, but also added another load of fertilizer (phosphate) to the already algae-clogged waters of America. Again, man had changed his environment without considering the possible consequences of his act.

The steadily increasing fertilization and death of water bodies resulted in yet another demand on the industry — "Get rid of the phosphate detergents." This was done with some products but at what cost to the environment no one knows at this time. Some of the most widely used substitute phosphate-free detergents may be more dangerous pollutants than either the suds or the phosphates. Some of them use a high percentage of caustic soda, which could upset the acid-alkali balance to the point where water would no longer sup-

It's no fun to play in a stream filled with detergent foam, garbage, or chemical wastes. It's also dangerous.

port life. Other substitutes use common table salt or plain baking soda, each with a potential pollution danger. The search goes on. In fact, everything has been tried except the most logical method — a return to soap — even if it does mean a loss in the whiteness of the household wash and bathtub ring.

The automobile, the main cause of air pollution, is also a large contributor to water pollution. As we learned in the section on air pollution, one of the exhaust wastes of the gasoline engine is nitrogen oxides. When combined with rain, these wastes form soluble nitrates which become additional fertilizers in the waterways of the nation.

Until recently, the farms and ranches of the nation did not contribute much to the pollution of water. Animal and plant wastes were used as fertilizers and soil builders. Irrigation was not widely used. In fact, most of the pollution resulting from farming and ranching occurred in the cities, where animals were slaughtered and inedible plant parts were discarded. Now this has changed, again with harmful consequences to the quality of the environment.

How do the farm and ranch contribute to water pollution?

After World War II, artificial fertilizers rich in phosphates and nitrates were produced in large quantities at low cost. Farmers, in their haste to increase crop production, used more fertilizer than their crops could absorb or the soil could hold. The excess fertilizer eventually washed into the streams and lakes to add to the already extensive water pollution problem.

Increasing construction of high dams and large artificial lakes made irrigation possible in many areas of the nation. The combination of cheap fertilizer and plentiful water for irrigation led to an increase in the salt content (salinity) of underground water supplies, as large amounts of the minerals contained in fertilizers leached (soaked) through the soil, and into the water supply. The salinity of the lower Colorado River, for example, is increasing yearly, and there is concern that the waters may soon be unfit for use by organisms that are adapted for living in or drinking fresh water.

Changed conditions in the cattle industry have had a considerable effect on water pollution. Cattle are now gathered in large fields called feed lots where they are fattened before slaughter for market. The natural balance of the range is lost. Wastes from masses of cattle on these feed lots make up much of the waste produced by domestic animals in the United States. It has been estimated that these animal wastes amount to more than ten times the amount of wastes produced by the human population. Up to this time, there has been no provision for treatment of these wastes. It's still the old attitude of "dump it in the river." But the costs to the environment are high. Some of the nation's most polluted streams are the result of man's methods of farming and marketing his products.

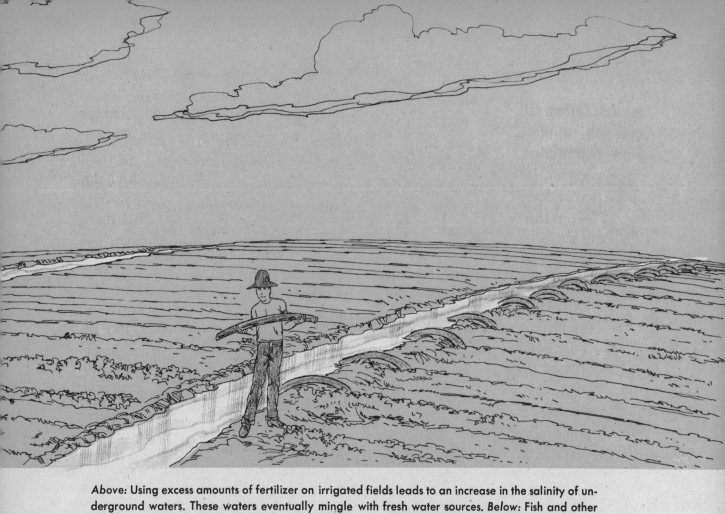

Above: Using excess amounts of fertilizer on irrigated fields leads to an increase in the salinity of underground waters. These waters eventually mingle with fresh water sources. *Below:* Fish and other organisms that are adapted for life in fresh water can die if the water supply becomes too salty.

The greatest contributors to water pollution are the factories, mills, and plants which produce our industrial products. There are many reasons for this. Industries have historically been located on a waterway because they used water in their manufacturing process (paper, steel) or used ships to bring in their raw materials and move out their manufactured products. Many industries are located on waterways because the waterways have always represented a free disposal area for their wastes. "Dump it into the lake or stream" was again the motto.

How does industry pollute water?

Now, the new concern for the quality of the environment has led many people to question the dumping of industrial wastes into the nation's waters. The problem is an enormous one. Every kind of industry produces, and dumps, some kind of pollutant. Paper mills dump fibers, dyes, and chemicals, including the poison mercury; steel mills dump acid wastes; petroleum spills have polluted waters and beaches in every section of the world; chemical plants dump every known chemical into our rivers, many of them poisonous to plants, animals, and man. Electric power plants are now producing a new kind of water pollution, thermal (heat) pollution, caused by the return of waste hot waters from the plant's cooling system to the water supply. Scientists are concerned that the heated waters may produce an environment that is unfit for fish and other water animals.

Restoring the quality of the water environments of the earth will be a costly as well as complex task. The only thing certain is that it must be done. The social, political, and economic battles which must be fought and won before this is accomplished will be discussed later, in the section, *The Environment and Society*.

During an oil spill the feathers of ducks and other water fowl become coated with oil and muck. If this coating is not cleaned off, death will result.

How are we polluting the land?

The United States has been called a "throw-away" society, and indeed we are. As a result, the nation is being buried under a pile of garbage, old papers, trash, automobiles, tires, cans, bottles, appliances, and the wastes of agriculture, business, and industry. For the unthinking and the lazy person, it has always seemed natural to litter. "Throw it out the car window," we say, and therefore, the

Above: Careless automobile riders and irresponsible advertisers make roads like this one all too common.

Below: The garbage that piles up on city streets during a sanitation strike is a menace to health. Uncovered garbage attracts a number of disease-carrying pests, including rats.

streets and highways of the nation are filled with litter.

There are four ways of getting rid of solid wastes — burn, bury, dump, or recycle. In our wasteful society, the logical method, recycling, or using again, has never been used, although other nations, such as Japan, have used our scrapped autos and steel to make their own high-grade steel. There is no reason why we cannot recycle much of our solid wastes, our paper, glass, aluminum, iron, and copper. Even our food wastes could be used to build soil in rural and desert areas by composting. The paper, glass, and aluminum industries have now begun a collection and recycling program.

In the meantime, the solid wastes pile up. In our urban areas, the amounts of solid waste are enormous. A strike by sanitation employees for only a few days can leave the city streets piled with garbage. It has been estimated that the solid wastes produced in the United States amount to over one billion pounds each day — or ten pounds for every urban resident and three pounds for every rural resident.

Disposal becomes more of a problem every day. For years, we have been dumping our waste products on the land, in swamps and coastal bays, and in the ocean. Dumping on the land, the centuries old method of solid waste disposal, is being restricted in most areas because of disease, odors, and general ugliness. Dumping in the swamps and estuaries or bays is also being restricted. San Francisco Bay dumping has been stopped, but not before 40 percent of the original bay had been filled in for home building and industry. New York has reached its limit here also. Part of Flushing Bay was filled in to make Flushing Meadow, site of the two New York World's Fairs and now the site of Shea Stadium, home of the Jets and Mets. Other cities are rapidly running out of dumping places. Burning by incineration has been restricted because of its contribution to air pollution.

What are we going to do? All of the disposal methods lead to some kind of environmental pollution and the nation is still unprepared for a major effort to recycle solid wastes. The social, economic, and political reasons for this will be explored later. At least, people are becoming aware of the problems of solid waste pollution, and some progress has been made. In addition to the new recycling programs for glass, aluminum, and paper, scientists are developing other new methods, including ultra-high temperature incinerators which leave little residue and air pollutants, composting techniques for sewage, and compacting (crushing) of autos, refrigerators and other materials into building blocks, which can be asphalt coated to seal out air and moisture. (However, these materials are lost for any further reuse.)

Indeed, our best hope is recycling or reuse of paper, glass, iron, copper, aluminum, and other scarce minerals. In addition to the elimination of major sources of solid waste pollution, recycling would ease the demands on some of the earth's vanishing mineral resources.

Noise! We cannot escape it, even in some of our most remote wilderness areas. Our homes are filled with the noise of television sets, radios, hi-fi's, food blenders, garbage disposal units, airconditioners, and vacuum cleaners. Outside the home, we hear aircraft, autos, trucks and buses, construction equipment, power boats and mowers, and portable radios. Snowmobiles, beach buggies, and dune carts invade the once quiet areas of the nation. Rock music played at the high decibel level many of its performers and listeners prefer, can temporarily, or in some cases permanently, impair

What is noise pollution?

hearing. Plans for supersonic airliners have been delayed, but not forgotten, and we can probably look forward to a future of sonic booms as these aircraft exceed the speed of sound. Even now, jet airports are surrounded by high-noise areas, whose inhabitants are subjected to intense noise pollution. John F. Kennedy airport in New York City, for example, affects an area of 25 square miles, and one side of it faces the open sea. An airport like O'Hare in Chicago, surrounded by community development, may affect an area twice that large.

The intensity of a sound is measured by a unit called a decibel. The decibel

These days, the silence of winter in the country is often shattered by the loud noise of a snowmobile.

The sounds made by a live rock band can reach 120 decibels, enough to cause pain and hearing impairment.

unit is logarithmic, which means that ten decibels are ten times as powerful as one decibel, 20 decibels are 100 times as powerful, 30 decibels are 1,000 times as powerful, and so on. The sound of rustling leaves is about 20 decibels, conversation about 60, heavy traffic about 90, a pneumatic jackhammer six feet away about 100, a jet airliner about 500 feet overhead measures 115 decibels, and the sound of a live rock band comes to about 120 decibels.

Sounds with a high decibel content are not only annoying, they are dangerous. A noise of only 85 decibels can produce some temporary hearing loss, and if the ears do not get a chance to recover, the impairment can become permanent. Most people experience actual pain when noise reaches 120 decibels, and deafness can result from exposure to sounds over 150 decibels. Noise can also produce irritability, tension, and nervous strain, and can elevate blood pressure and raise the amount of cholesterol in the blood, thus contributing to heart trouble. The danger of noise pollution has only recently been recognized. But now that the problem has been recognized it is up to all

The delayed radiation, or fallout, from an atomic blast may occur years after the actual explosion.

What is radiation pollution?

The manufacture and testing of atomic weapons added a new pollution problem to the world environment, the threat of radiation from uranium and manufactured radioactive materials. Recognizing the radiation dangers, some nations have curtailed the open-air testing of atomic devices, but the danger of underground test radiation still exists. Atom-powered electric plants increase the radiation pollution of the atmosphere, as well as of waterways, since the problems of radioactive waste disposal have not yet been resolved.

In spite of these threats to the quality of the environment, public demand for more electricity makes it fairly obvious that atomic plants represent the only immediate solution to the power supply problem. The alternative is increased use of coal for power production, with the resultant increase in other kinds of pollution.

Once again, the complexity of the problems and the difficulty of solutions arise. We demand more power. We demand a cleaner environment. We demand all the benefits of technology, but are unwilling to accept the natural consequences of our actions. As with all the other pollution problems, man is being forced to make some difficult choices, choices that may mean a significant change in his life style and standard of living. Is man willing to cut down on the use of cars, electricity, and the noise of technology in order to have a better environment? Are you?

of us — politicians who pass laws, industrialists with noisy plants, manufacturers who make noisy products, and individuals who thoughtlessly add to the noise in the air by sounding horns excessively, playing radios at top volume, etc. — to do something about the problem.

Poisons

Man the hunter, man the gardener, even man the small farmer, learned to live with the natural enemies of his plants and animals — the predators, the insects, and the disease-producing bacteria and fungi. Small amounts of poisons were used to control some insects which caused crop damage. However, as farms became larger and agriculture changed from general crop production to single crop production, insects multiplied enormously. They found mile after mile of corn or wheat, mile after mile of cotton, mile after mile of orchards. All the insects had to do was eat and multiply. Man did not want to share his food with the increased insect population, and used poisons against them, but was never successful in controlling his insect enemies.

Then, during World War II, DDT and other chlorinated hydrocarbons were produced and used to control flies, mosquitoes, lice, and other insects. DDT was the answer to the prayers of public health officials. After the war, it became the savior of the farmer, the fruit grower, the forester, and the mosquito control agencies. DDT was effective, it was cheap and easy to produce, and it was persistent — it lasted a long time in the environment. Other poisons similar to DDT were produced to control termites, ants, and rodents. The earth was literally covered with sprays of DDT and various other chlorinated hydrocarbons.

Within a few years, bird lovers and wildlife biologists became concerned. **What happened to the birds?** Robins were found dead on lawns where elm trees had been sprayed to control Dutch elm disease. The populations of hawks, owls, and even our national bird, the bald eagle, declined sharply. Scientists suspected DDT, but there was no proof until DDT was found in the fatty tissues of dead birds, fish, and animals. Eggs of hawks and eagles contained large amounts of DDT. It was found in cranberries. It was even found in the bodies of Antarctic penguins and seals. DDT used on the farms and forests of America to control insect enemies had spread around the earth. It was everywhere, and people began to demand an end to its use. Other less persistant poisons have been developed, but they are still poisons, and they too, kill or destroy the animals which feed on the poisoned insects.

As with all of our environmental problems, the solutions are complex and difficult. It is evident that in this age of food scarcity around the world, we cannot afford to share our crops with hordes of insects. Neither can we afford to fill the bodies of all life on earth with poisons, the effects of which we do not fully understand. In fact, many scientists are concerned about the effect of DDT on the tiny algae in the oceans which produce most of the food

The bald eagle, symbol of the U.S., is an endangered species. DDT, found in the tissues of eagles and other dead birds, is one of the reasons. The eagle absorbs DDT through its food, mainly fish and dead animals.

and oxygen available for living things. (DDT is believed to interfere with the food-making process, or photosynthesis, of algae.) So, the search goes on for safer methods of insect and disease control, such as trying to sterilize insects, or using natural enemies against them.

In the meantime, however, while new methods are being perfected, our use of poisons for insect control continues. Although the use of DDT has been reduced, and in some states (Michigan, Wisconsin and New York) banned, the use of other persistent chlorinated hy-

drocarbons still goes on. Also, ever-increasing amounts of DDT and similar poisons are shipped abroad for use in insect control in developing countries. Is this intelligent? If the DDT sprayed on the crops and trees of America found its way into the fatty tissues of Antarctic penguins, isn't it naive to think that DDT used on crops in India, the Philippines, and other nations will not find its way back into the United States? Once again, the problems are complex. Certainly, the peoples of the world need more food. But do they need it at the cost of poisoning all life on earth?

"Swordfish is contaminated with mercury," says the news commentator. Where did the mercury come from, and how did it get into the swordfish? Like the DDT in the oceans, mercury, and many other deadly poisons like it, have been dumped in the waters

How do chemicals hurt the environment?

Ladybird beetles (or ladybugs) are the natural enemies of many insects that destroy crops and gardens.

of the world by industries that use these poisons in their manufacturing processes. Mercury was long thought to be an inert substance, that is, a chemical which does not easily combine with other chemicals or substances. In 1970, it was discovered that bacterial action allowed mercury to combine with several substances to form highly poisonous compounds, which were since found in large numbers of game birds and animals, fish, and sea animals.

Since the recent alarms about mercury poisoning, most but not all mercury discharges have been reduced, and we can look forward to an end to the dumping of mercury wastes into the environment. However, the mercury already dumped will cause problems for years to come, and many other poisons — arsenic, cyanides, lead, etc. — are still being dumped into the waters and on the land by industries which use them in their manufacturing processes. With our new concern for the quality of the environment, industry will have to find a new, safe method for the disposal of poisonous wastes.

Poverty of the Environment

One of the most serious problems of the environment is the steadily diminishing quality of the resources on which man depends for his survival on earth — soil, water, forests, grasslands, wildlife, minerals, and open space for recreation. Until recently, no thought was given to either the quality or the future supply of these vital resources. Now our concern is a real and growing one. We have squandered our rich heritage of resources by exploitation and waste. Let us examine each of these resources briefly.

The loss of soil was first brought to the attention of the general public in the 1930s when great clouds of soil — dust storms — arose in the dust-

How is soil being lost?

bowl in the Midwestern states, and eventually covered over 50,000,000 acres of land. Whole farms in the great plains area blew away following removal of the protective grass covering which had held the soil in place for centuries. Periodic droughts dried the now uncovered farm lands, and winds carried the dried-out soil away. In the South, the same thing was happening to the lands which were left bare of their cover to raise cotton. Here the light, exposed soil was washed away, leaving deep gullies of unusable land. In the West and Southwest, overgrazing by large herds of cattle and sheep removed the protective grass cover, leaving near desert conditions behind.

Not all soil losses have been due to erosion (washing or blowing away).

When the natural plant cover that holds topsoil in place is overgrazed by cattle or sheep or plowed under in order to raise crops, erosion can take place. *Above:* In windy areas, the exposed topsoil gradually dries out. Then, the next strong wind can cause a duststorm. *Below:* If it rains on lands left bare of plant cover, topsoil can be washed away, leaving behind unusable land cut with deep channels called gullies.

Much of the best farmland in America has been covered by cities, airports, highways, shopping centers — in short, by asphalt. The grass planted along the new interstate highway system to control erosion and contribute to beautification is not used for any other purpose. It alone could feed millions of cattle.

Some of the most fertile valleys have been covered by reservoirs to produce electricity and irrigation water. And these benefits will prove temporary, for silt carried into these reservoirs by the swiftly-flowing water will eventually fill every one of them and make them worthless for power and water storage.

Another cause of soil loss is alkalinity (increase of salt content) due to excessive use of fertilizers and irrigation water. Extensive areas of once productive soil in Idaho, California, and Arizona are rapidly becoming useless alkali (salt) flats as minerals from fertilizer are washed into them.

Soil loss goes on at an expanded rate. Where will it end? Where will man grow the food and fiber necessary for our expanding population? Indeed, how long can we go on feeding our present population?

Pollution of the nation's waters has already been discussed.

How are we losing water? But even if the pollution of our rivers, lakes, and streams could be eliminated

Dams do provide irrigation water and help produce electric power. But they also flood millions of tillable acres of land with the waters that accumulate behind the dam in a reservoir.

Forests once covered most of the world, including all of North America.

or at least greatly reduced, there would still be problems of water supply, especially in areas of high population density and low yearly rainfall. The demand for water for all uses increases daily. Underground water supplies are being depleted in many areas, as pumping exceeds the amount of recharge (water soaking back into the soil). Where this pumping is accompanied by irrigation, as in Arizona, underground waters are becoming salty from minerals carried into the soil by the irrigation water. Even in high rainfall areas, underground water levels are diminishing as more water falls on asphalt and is quickly carried away, instead of soaking into the ground. In coastal areas like Atlantic City, New Jersey and southern California, there is a danger of salt water from the oceans coming in to replace the natural fresh water in the earth.

Little remains of the extensive virgin forests that covered much of the United States before 1800, and plans are being made to harvest most of the remaining virgin timber stands. Only the forests of the National Parks and the National Wilderness System will escape the power saws. Many foresters are con-

Why are the virgin forests disappearing?

27

vinced that *all* forests should be managed. Old trees should be cut down and replaced with young trees, which grow faster. These foresters refer to old trees as overmature. To people concerned about the future of our forests they say, "Don't worry, there is more wood being produced each year than is being harvested." That is true, but the big trees which are producing our best grade of lumber will be no more. Management plans will call for a tree to be cut long before it becomes large and overmature. People who enjoy seeing the big trees are upset to think of future forests in which there will be no large trees.

Where is all the new wood production? A good deal of it is in the South, where the wood is used mostly for paper. Certainly these young trees are growing rapidly, but where will we go for quality lumber when the last virgin forests of the Northwest and Alaska are gone?

Foresters have come under attack recently for the degradation of the environment caused by a harvest method known as clear-cutting, in which every tree in a section is cut. The goal of this kind of management is an even-aged stand of trees which will be easier and more economical to harvest. Clear-cutting is also necessary in order to grow trees like Douglas fir, cherry, and black walnut, all valuable commercially, which will not grow in the shade of

Some forests are cut selectively—taking a few trees from an area and then replanting bare spots. But oth-

ers are harvested by means of clear-cutting, which leaves a once-healthy forest a grove of stumps.

Grasslands can be destroyed by plowing the land for agriculture, or by overgrazing.

other trees. In areas of high rainfall and long growing seasons like those of the Pacific northwest, new trees soon cover the clear-cut area. But in cold sections of the Rocky Mountains like Montana and Colorado, where growing seasons are only a few months at best, clear-cut forests will take many, many years to grow again. Other people are questioning clear-cutting for esthetic reasons. "Clear-cut areas are a mess and must be eliminated," they say. West Virginia has banned all clear-cutting in the state and Montana is considering similar action.

Here again, the solutions are complex. Everyone has a different reason for loving the forest. It used to be that a forester measured a tree to determine its value as lumber or pulp. Now he must also consider whether it is a home for wildlife, a place on which to hang a swing, or a model for an artist painting it. Which has the greater value? Regardless of how that question is answered, the forests of the future will be used and managed with more attention to how they contribute to the beauty, as well as the bounty of the nation. Fortunately, forests are a renewable resource and, unless destroyed, will continue to supply man with lumber, paper, and a myriad of other products as well as places for recreation and wildlife.

As we learned in the section on soil, the original grass-

What happened to the grasslands? lands of America have been nearly lost, with the exception of the ranges in

29

the West and Southwest. Even these are in poor condition due to overgrazing, low rainfall, and exploitation. Of course, the midwest grasslands are now the great corn and wheat producing farms which supply the nation with most of its cereal grains.

Some of the dustbowl areas of the Great Plains have been reestablished as prairie lands. They are now called the National Grasslands, and will be protected forever from the plow and cultivation. However, much more needs to be done. The poor condition of the range lands of the West represents a striking example of the increasing poverty of the environment in America. Much effort and vast sums of money will' be needed to restore them to the quality they once had.

As man extended his range, or living area, the great variety of wildlife diminished. Wolves and mountain lions were once found over most of the United States. Bears were widespread. Elk roamed the eastern forests. Millions of buffalo and pronghorn

What has man done to the wildlife around him?

roamed the great prairie grasslands of the midwest. Prairie-dog towns covered many square miles, and the blackfooted ferrets (a type of weasel) which preyed on them, were numerous. Eagles, hawks, and owls helped to keep the populations of rodents in check.

Then man cut down the forests of the east and north central states, and of the Appalachian Mountains. The grasslands were plowed under for cereal crop production, or overgrazed by cattle and sheep.

The natural predators of man's farm animals were ruthlessly exterminated. State governments paid bounties for the killing of foxes, coyotes, wolves, mountain lions, hawks, and owls. Even today, the killing of predators goes on. Man's campaign to exterminate the wily coyote has cost the government millions of dollars. Man has spread poison over the western home of the coyote, and has used every kind of trap and killing device. The coyote still survives, but its numbers are greatly reduced.

Ranchers spread poisoned bait for the coyote because they fear his ability to prey on livestock. But the coyote's preferred diet, mostly rodents and carrion, actually helps ranchers.

Now, however, man is discovering that the coyote provided a valuable service to the rancher who tried to kill him — he kept the rodents in check. Without the coyote, ranches are being overrun by rodents which eat the seed and forage on which the rancher's livestock depend for food.

In addition to the killing of predators in the misguided belief that he was saving his farm and ranch animals, man directly killed many birds and animals for sport or profit. Buffalo were shot from trains for "sport" until they were almost extinct. Passenger pigeons were shot by the millions for market, until they *did* become extinct. Egrets were nearly exterminated by men seeking the plume feathers to adorn ladies' hats.

The harp seal pup is born with beautiful white fur. Trying to obtain this fur (used to make fashionable men's and women's coats), hunters go after the pups with clubs. Sometimes the club only stuns the pup, not killing it, and the baby seal is skinned alive.

Passenger pigeons are a species that became extinct because of man's greed. The last one died in 1914.

Fur seals and sea otters were nearly wiped out, and beaver and other fur-bearing animals became scarce as men sought their furs for coats. On a world-wide scale, the beautiful cats — the tigers, leopards, jaguars and cheetahs — are still being hunted for their fur, and whales for their oil and ambergris, even though continued hunting threatens these species with extinction. The list of endangered species, that is, forms of wildlife in danger of extinction by man, reached 900 in 1970, according to the World Wildlife Fund.

Official figures for the commercial catch of lake herring in Lake Erie dropped from 835,000 pounds in 1950 to practically none in 1970. Doesn't it seem that man would have suspected long before now that Lake Erie was dying? Will we destroy all our other fish and wildlife resources as well? Although steps are being taken to set aside space for wildlife, the loss of wildlife land to highways, housing, and industry continues at a rate of over one million acres a year. With our expanding population, this loss of essential homes for wildlife may well increase despite all our efforts and good intentions. And even if the land can be saved, wildlife faces a very uncertain future because of the poisons and other pollutants in the environment.

By studying the production, use, and supply of minerals, we can see the best example of the increasing poverty of the environment. Let us investigate some of the problems associated with our search for extraction, use, and reuse of minerals.

What are we doing about minerals?

The search for new mineral sources has been intensified in recent years as man slowly came to the realization that the mineral resources of the earth are being rapidly depleted. These resources, unlike trees, cannot be replaced. This intensified search has caused new problems and controversy, because the search has extended into previously untouched wilderness areas such as the White Clouds area in the Sawtooth Mountains of Idaho, and the north slope of the Brooks Range in Alaska, where vast oil fields have been discovered. The problem in each case is how to get the minerals out of the ground and to market without destroying large parts of man's remaining wild habitat.

Why does man need to go into these environmentally valuable regions for minerals? Recent estimates indicate that the United States uses over 30 percent of the world's minerals, and supplies are becoming limited. U.S. estimated reserves, at the present rate of use, will last as follows:

crude oil	–	30 years
natural gas	–	15 years
uranium	–	30 years
lead	–	52 years
coal	–	1,000 years

We cannot depend on other countries to supply our needs, since many nations are demanding nationalization and home use of their mineral (as well as timber, fish, etc.) resources.

As a nation, we waste our minerals disgracefully. We do not use iron and steel scrap, yet they are the metallic equivalent of pig iron. The Japanese steel industry cheaply buys up the scrap we throw away, and then uses it in its processing plants. In the United States, we use over one and a half tons of iron ore, one ton of coke, and a half ton of limestone to make one ton of pig iron. All of this could be saved by using scrap.

Why don't we do it? Again, the answers are complex. We are still a nation of wasters, big spenders. It is still cheaper, with government depletion allowances, to use new iron ore than to process scrap. It is deemed economically more efficient to throw the scrap away or let the Japanese outproduce us with it. We must start to recycle our steel and iron scrap. We can also save a

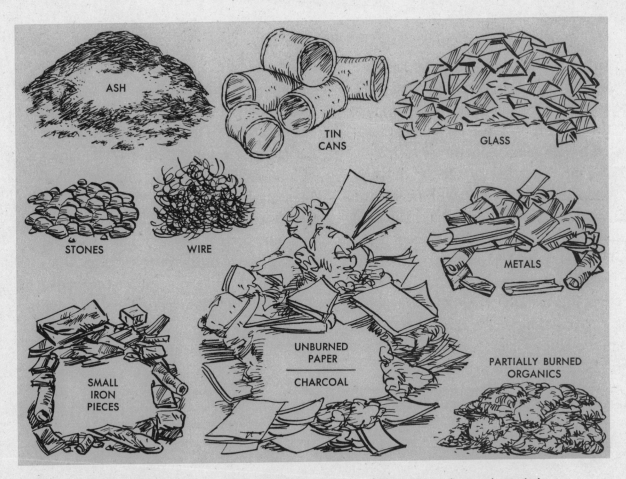

ASH

TIN CANS

GLASS

STONES

WIRE

METALS

SMALL IRON PIECES

UNBURNED PAPER
—
CHARCOAL

PARTIALLY BURNED ORGANICS

Trash usually contains potentially valuable waste. It should be separated out and recycled.

great deal of our mineral resources by better use of mine ore waste, and by reclamation of the wasted minerals thrown out on ore heaps because it was uneconomical to extract them from the rock. We use only the high-grade ore, the rest we throw away.

There is hope that the new ultra-high temperature incinerators may contribute to the solution of this waste problem. With all organic materials burned up, the residue can be recycled to separate the iron, non-iron metal, and glass. It has been estimated that a ton of this incinerator residue would yield a half ton of glass, 700 pounds of iron, and 50 pounds of other metals.

Perhaps man's greatest contribution to the pollution and poverty of the environment has been his actions in extracting coal from the earth. Deep mining had its harmful effects, particularly from the drainage of acid into the soil (produced when water which fills old mines reacts with chemicals in the mine to form acid and then drains back into the soil). Damage was also caused by the coal mines in Pennsylvania, in which fires have been burning along a coal seam for a century. But in strip-mining, man has created the most potent monster of environmental destruction ever devised. For shallow coal seams, man found it cheaper and easier to strip off the top surface, extract the coal, and leave behind the stripped land, a new environment which can support only one thing — poverty. Ancient mining laws allow coal operators to follow the coal wherever it goes, through towns, homes, or farms, with no regard to ownership. Only rarely have the coal operators reclaimed the stripped land. Although penalties for leaving the land stripped are imposed by local governments, it is usually cheaper for the operator to pay the penalty than to rehabilitate the land.

Several states are trying to abolish strip-mining, but the demands for coal are so great that such a goal will be difficult to attain. The U.S. Department of the Interior estimates that reclamation of land ravaged by strip-mining in Appalachia alone would cost 250 million dollars. Acids and sediments have contaminated an estimated ten thousand miles of once-clear trout streams. Piles of soil and rocks removed from above the coal seams slide in avalanches down the mountain slopes, burying everything below. "Total destruction," say the resi-

Strip mining has destroyed over two million acres of land. Huge power shovels remove the layer of earth and rock that covers the coal seam. The exposed coal is removed with smaller power shovels, leaving the scarred earth behind. Many coal companies prefer to pay a small fine rather than reclaim the damaged land.

dents of Appalachia. "Total Benefit Industry," reads the title of one coal company's publication, extolling the benefits of a few newly-made water holes which offer boating, fishing, and recreation to the residents who live in poverty.

The problems are being recognized, but they can only increase. The national demand for coal increases yearly, and there is still an estimated 100 billion tons of strippable coal remaining. Strip-mining operators are looking at huge deposits in Utah, Arizona, Wyoming, Montana, and North Dakota now that legislators in Appalachia have tough-ened regulations on their operations. Will we create other Appalachias in these new areas? Is the coal worth the cost to the environment?

Even with the best, most economic, most efficient use, new mineral resources will run out in the near future. We must use and reuse what we have. When our minerals are gone, they will be gone forever.

The problems of urban environments are probably **What is happening to our cities?** causing more concern than any other. Every problem previously

mentioned in this section is compounded in the city. The air is dirtier, the water is more polluted, wildlife is almost nonexistent, and wastes continue to pile up faster than they can be removed. Big cities have been completely paralyzed by a few days of mail strikes, sanitation strikes, transportation strikes, or strikes by truck drivers who deliver the products on which the city depends.

Still, Americans pour into the great urban areas seeking better opportunities than they could find in their native rural surroundings. As a result, 70 percent of the population lives on less than 10 percent of the land. Cities have spread so rapidly that it is sometimes difficult to tell where one ends and another begins. The megalopolis, a densely populated area that surrounds a city, extends from Boston to Washington, from Buffalo to Milwaukee, north, south, and east of Los Angeles, around the entire coast of Florida (except for Everglades National Park), and from Dallas-Fort Worth to Houston.

With conditions of poverty in all its aspects facing every urban area in America, how can the increased populations expected by the year 2000 be accommodated? What kind of standard of living will urban inhabitants face? Will the migration reverse itself and take people back to the open spaces? Can we build new cities in new environ-

Right: Cities have spread out so much it is sometimes hard to tell where one stops and another begins.

The cry of "Go West, young man!" inspired pioneers in the 1800s. But there is no Western land left. Where do we go from here?

ments? Do we want to? Can we afford to destroy and rebuild a whole series of urban areas? Will we do what the colonial farmers did when their farms failed — move west to new cities? And are there new lands that will support urban population complexes? These are some of the questions which must be answered, and answered quickly.

As with all environmental problems, the urban crisis will not be resolved easily. Some urban planners feel that even with large expenditures of money, the cities are doomed. They feel that the nation must look to new cities to accommodate the masses of people who need housing. The population in this country is expected to double by the year 2000. This means that during the next 30 years we must produce the same number of dwelling units that now presently exist! Where will these housing units be built? There is no land-use plan, or even a land-use policy to guide the location and distribution of the new growth in the nation. Without such a policy and plan, we will continue our present course of haphazard growth which has had such a terrible impact on the total environment of America.

While population is blamed by many for the present ills of the environment, it is well to remember that much of the environmental destruction in this country was accomplished when our national population was much smaller. In our mad rush to grow, we squandered our resources and polluted our world. Now we must face up to the consequences. Certainly, any increases in population will make the job of environmental rehabilitation more difficult. Changes in our style of living must take place. A continuation of our present course of contributing to the poverty of the environment will probably lead to man's destruction. Just as our endangered species of wildlife declined in numbers when their habitat was destroyed, so man will decline in numbers, and in health, if he continues to destroy his habitat — the earth.

Population

Population, the last of the "P" problems to be discussed, is of great concern to many scientists and environmentalists. In 1650, the population of the world was about 500 million people. By 1850, this figure had doubled. The population more than doubled again by 1950, and in 1971, it rose to over three and a half billion people.

The world population is expected to double again by the year 2000, and some scientists and other experts feel that earth cannot support this amount of people. They fear there will not be enough food to feed them, or space available to house them. In order to understand more fully the problem of overpopulation, we must first study the basic rules which govern all life on earth.

How the Environment Works

In order to understand how the environment works, it is necessary to investigate the three basic rules which govern life on earth:

Change — all living things and all environments constantly change, and each change creates a new environment.

Interdependence — all living things are interdependent with each other and with their environment.

Interaction — living things, and populations of living things, are the result of interaction between species (inherited) factors and environmental factors.

There are many kinds of changes which affect living things and their environment. Most important, because all life is dependent on them, are the natural cycles which govern the substances that make up all living things, the four basic elements of the environment: carbon, oxygen, hydrogen, and nitrogen. All of these cycles are driven by the energy of the sun.

What is the rule of change?

In the process called photosynthesis (or putting together with light), the sun's energy is captured by the green plants of the land and water and used to convert carbon dioxide and water into food, fiber, and fuel. During this process, oxygen is produced — the oxygen which is necessary to the life activities of all living things. Plants also incorporate nitrogen into the basic food manufacturing process to make pro-

The sun's energy passes through a food chain. The energy is stored by primary producers, green plants. These are eaten by primary consumers, grazing animals such as cattle and sheep. They are eaten by secondary consumers, carnivores such as man, who still benefit from the energy stored in the original green plant.

teins, on which all animal life depends for its existence (already the interdependence of all living things is becoming apparent). Animals then eat plant-produced materials to supply their energy, and in turn give off the carbon dioxide, nitrates, and phosphates on which plant life depends. This is the basic cycle of life — the oxygen-carbon dioxide cycle.

Other natural cycles are constantly redistributing the nitrogen-protein materials. We see these processes going on all the time, as seeds sprout, plants grow, produce seeds, die, and return to the environment through decomposition, to be reused by plants to make more protein.

There is a third cycle, which may be called the cycle of resource and waste. In the natural environment, every waste becomes a resource for another living thing. Our waste food materials, for example, become resources for other liv-

ing things after they have decayed. In the early days of this nation when the population was small, even human and animal wastes served as fertilizers for plants. Wood rotted, animal bodies decayed, paper and cloth disintegrated, all to be used again. Now, man has produced so much waste that it accumulates into enormous masses. The natural processes of decay cannot take care of the wastes of man, not even his organic wastes. As a result, we have pollution.

As change goes on during these great natural cycles, there is a constant exchange of energy. We may consider the earth as a great, closed reservoir of energy — a closed ecosystem. Like a reservoir of water, the energy reservoir has a source of supply (an inlet) and a demand for withdrawal (an outlet). These must be in near balance. Green plants constantly put energy into the earth energy reservoir. The energy is used by animals and man to run their

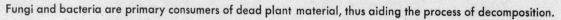

Fungi and bacteria are primary consumers of dead plant material, thus aiding the process of decomposition.

bodies (food), to fuel their fires, and to run their factories (fuel — coal, oil, and wood).

At the present time, there is not enough energy (food and fuel) in the earth's reservoir. Millions of people are starving; a much larger number are continually hungry. Many of those with enough to eat are lacking in the proteins essential to healthy bodies. And predictions indicate a greatly increased world population and greatly increased demands for food energy. At the same time, large areas once covered by energy producing (and oxygen producing) plants are being taken out of production in order to make way for man's other needs — housing, highways for transportation, etc. How low can we let the earth's energy reservoir go? Do we already have too many people on earth? Can we even hope to feed a doubled world population? Could we feed a doubled population in the U.S. and still maintain our dietary standards?

So far, we have been talking about natural changes in living things and their earth environment. But man has changed even the order of change. Man is the principal agent of change in the modern environment. Man decides whether living things and environments survive. Man can decide to cut down the forest, kill all the endangered species, destroy or protect his environment. Unfortunately, man has failed to realize that each of the changes he has introduced into the environment has a consequence — a changed environment. So man introduced DDT and other poisons without considering the conse-

quences. He introduced detergents. He made steel and paper without thinking of the consequences of his use of resources or the wastes he created. He destroyed wildlife habitats. Now he has allowed himself to multiply beyond the capacity of the environment to support his numbers.

If man can learn to anticipate and predict the consequences of his actions on the environment, he may yet be able to avoid the danger to his survival. Indications are, man *is* learning to do this. The SST (*supersonic transport* plane) development was defeated in this country because of its possible consequences to the environment. The Alaskan pipeline which will carry oil from the North Slope fields is being carefully studied to avoid possible harmful consequences to the land it must go through. Isn't it too bad that man took so long to learn this fundamental law of change and consequence to the environment?

Living things depend on their environment. Think of what you ate for breakfast, or the clothes you are wearing. You probably did not grow your own food, or make your own clothes. You are dependent on your environment and other people, and other living things, for the food you eat, the energy you need to walk and run, the clothes you wear, and everything you do. You are dependent on the resources of the earth, its water, its soil, its forests. That is why the quality of the environment is so important to you and to all of life.

What is the rule of interdependence?

41

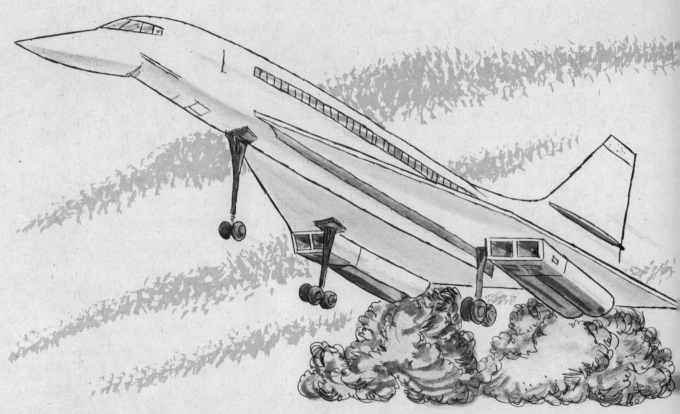

The gigantic engines on supersonic transport planes may raise airplane noise to a new, intolerable high. For this reason, Congress voted to delay SST production in order to study the consequences to the environment.

Just as you and all living things are dependent on the environment, the environment is dependent on you and other living things. If man pollutes or exploits resources, or wastes, or makes harmful changes in the environment, the environment will suffer a loss of quality and a lessening of resources. A healthy environment, an environment of beauty and bounty, is one in which the natural laws are allowed to operate without too much disturbance. We have seen the consequences when the natural operation of the environment is altered. We do not have to eliminate change. Instead, we have to initiate change which will have beneficial consequences, not harmful ones. Up until very recently, man considered himself to be the ruler of the natural world. Now he is learning that he is just as interdependent with it as any other living thing, plant or animal. The warning to man is clear. If man destroys his environment, he will destroy himself, because he is dependent on the environment and it in turn is dependent on him.

How do living things interact with their

What is the rule of interaction?

environment? Every living thing has certain traits or characteristics with which it was born — which it inherited from its parents, be they plant, animal, or man. If heredity was the only factor needed to determine what each human would become, making predictions about individuals would be easy. But the environment affects each individual throughout his or her life. Let us see how this works.

If there were two identical twin girls, their genetic inheritance, and therefore, their traits, would be similar at birth. Two sisters or even two fraternal (non-identical) twins would be different, since their genetic makeup may be similar, but is not exactly the same, as in the case of identical twins. Now suppose these two identical twins were 13 years old. Environmental factors, things that happened to them in their environment, might make them very different individuals. For example, one may have had pneumonia (disease), broken an arm (accident), taken drugs (social factor), or eaten less than her twin. Would they still be the same? Of course not. One might be entirely different than the

other. And though they have the same features, they might even look different, since they might choose different hair, makeup, and clothes styles. So it is with all living things. The individual is constantly reacting, or interacting, with elements of its environment — food, shelter, disease, accident, drugs, other individuals, or natural happenings such as weather, fire, or floods.

Why is this important to our study of the environment? Because, as we have learned, when man makes changes of any kind in the environment, he introduces new environmental factors with which the individual must interact. For example, we have all eaten DDT or mercury in our food, inhaled carbon monoxide and lead, been crowded, subjected to noise, etc. How will our bodies react? Will we be strong enough to

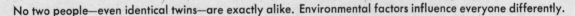

No two people—even identical twins—are exactly alike. Environmental factors influence everyone differently.

resist the effects of poison? Will we become deaf from too much noise? Will we be able to breathe in the polluted air? How we react will determine whether or not we survive. It is the same for all other living things.

Populations are determined by the same natural laws of interaction between species and environmental factors. In the case of human and animal populations, the species factors are those which increase populations (production), and the environmental factors are those which reduce or limit them. Here is how it works.

Why should we control population growth?

Species factors which increase populations are:

1. Number of offspring — the more young that are produced, the bigger the population.
2. Care of young — the more care, the better the chances of survival and the bigger the population.
3. Length of life — the longer the species lives, the bigger the population.
4. Age of reproduction — the sooner the young are able to reproduce, the more individuals will be added to the population.
5. Length of reproductive life — the more years during which young are produced, the bigger the population.

When a deer population outgrows the food supply, food becomes a limiting factor. The deer population in this forest has eaten all twigs and leaves within reach, and must now move on or starve to death.

You can see that if there were no other factors, the species that produced the most offspring over the longest period and took care of its young to insure survival, would have the biggest population. Now let us examine the environmental factors which reduce populations, the population limiting factors:

1. Food — only a certain number of individuals can live on a given supply of food.

2. Shelter — most living things require some kind of shelter from the environment or their enemies.

3. Enemies — those that live on the species; that eat them or use them for other purposes.

4. Weather — a cold winter, for example, can result in many deaths (even human).

5. Natural disasters — fire, flood, earthquake, etc.

6. Disease — other living things that live in, or at the expense of, the species, such as parasites, bacteria, or viruses.

7. Space — most living things need space (a territory) for living, feeding, nesting, etc.

8. Poisons — chemicals which kill or reduce the ability to reproduce, such as DDT.

Although each and all of these factors in the environment may operate to keep a population of living things in balance, usually one of these factors is the important one in controlling a population. This one is called the limiting factor. With most living things, food is the limiting factor. In the long run, food will probably be the environmental factor that will limit the human population. Unless, of course, man poisons his whole environment first.

Consider how man has tried to elimi-

In earlier times, disease was more of a limiting factor for the human population. Epidemics of bubonic plague, cholera, and smallpox killed thousands, and the sight of the dead being carted away used to be a common one.

nate the environmental factors which tend to reduce his numbers. He has made many common diseases avoidable or curable. He has reduced the effects of his natural enemies, the insects, diseases, and animals which compete with him for his food and fiber. He has built shelters that protect him against his enemies, weather conditions, and many natural disasters. Because he overcame many of the limiting factors, man's population has grown at an alarming rate. Only in his attempts to supply himself with food has man been somewhat unsuccessful. Now, with his increasing population, he may also be running out of space in which to live and still keep enough land in crops and fiber. Indeed, man's population must soon be brought into balance with his available resources. If it is not done by his own de-

sign and planning, it will be done by some one of the environmental factors — the limiting factor — with extremely unpleasant consequences.

Man has been most successful in pro-

Can technology help the environment? ducing the material goods he needs. His inventions and machines have made remarkable progress possible — progress in transportation, agriculture, industry, and communications. Man has walked on the moon, sent scientific instruments to collect data from the stars. Technology has become so important that advances in technology have been equated with advances in progress. Growth is used as an indicator of success. The United States is the richest nation in the world because of its

Our technology has advanced enough for us to land a man on the moon. When will we advance enough to use technology to better the environment, to make the quality of life on earth more pleasant?

technology. Yet the quality of life in this country is not always pleasant. Why?

We have overlooked the fact that technology is only a tool, not an end in itself. In the past, technology has been used to accumulate material wealth at the expense of a polluted environment. When we consider the cost of steel, or paper, or chemicals, we do not take into account the cost of waste disposal. Waste disposal has always been free. People concerned about the quality of the environment are realizing that technology must be made to work for the environment, not against it. Using technology to increase economic return at the expense of the environment is so much a part of our national existence that the solutions to the "P" problems will require changes in our life styles, economy, relations with other nations, and the total philosophy of resource use, but it must be done. If our wealth and productivity are dependent on the quality of the environment and the continuous supply of its resources, then the cost of maintaining an environment of quality must be considered of utmost importance.

The quality of the environment can no longer be sacrificed to accommodate productivity. Man must now make some difficult decisions. Up to now, the decisions were easy. They were always decided on the basis of production and economics. Now the decisions must be made on the basis of the future quality of the environment. Instead of using technology to develop a more profitable car or detergent, we must use it to develop pollution-free products. More technical know-how must be devoted to the problem of sewage treatment. The list could go on and on, but the fact remains — the quality of the environment must be the basic determiner of productivity and economic growth if we are to continue to exist. How could we have overlooked this simple fact of interdependence for so long and at such a terrible price to the future of life on earth?

How does man reach a decision regarding his use of a resource or his actions toward other living things and his environment? As we have seen, man has not called upon scientists to predict the possible effects of his actions. Science should be basic to any decision affecting the physical and biological world. The geologist is the only one who can accurately predict oil reserves. Populations of living things can only be predicted by biologists who have studied the species and environmental factors which affect them. Only chemists and physicians can predict the effects of poisons, chemical additives and other substances introduced into the environment. Soil scientists can tell us what we must do to avoid tragic losses of topsoil to erosion or salinity. Foresters have the knowledge to manage the forest resources to insure a continuous yield of high quality timber. Through our knowledge of genetics, we can produce bigger, more productive, disease free crops of food plants and trees.

Can science help the environment?

47

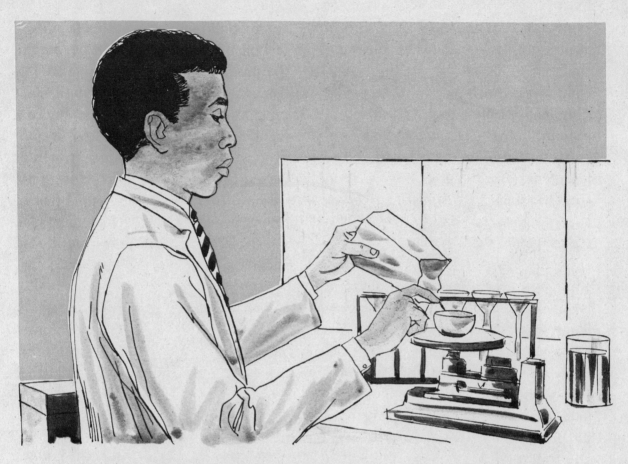

Soil scientists study the characteristics and behavior of soil and try to increase its productivity.

Indeed, man has the scientific knowledge to solve most of the problems which are causing our crisis in the environment. We know how to eliminate the pollution of the air and water; we know how to eliminate the poisons which are dangerous to life on earth. We have all the knowledge to bring the population of the earth into balance with the resources of the earth, and maintain that population. We know how to do the same thing for wildlife, so as to insure its survival and continued role in the delicate balance of energy and resource cycling.

With adequate funding of basic scientific research, scientists could find the answers to the still unanswered problems. Is there a substitute for the internal combustion engine? Can the sonic boom be eliminated or lessened? Can we reduce noise? Can our food production and storage capabilities be increased? Can we find a way of dissipating the heat from electric power generation? If we can put a man on the moon, we can do all of these other things. Isn't our survival and the maintenance of our standard of living enough incentive? These are the questions which must be answered. They can all be reduced to one big query: "Why don't we do it?" Perhaps we can find some of the answers to these questions in the next section, *The Environment and Society.*

The Environment and Society

Why don't we use our scientific knowledge to solve the problems of the environment? As we have learned, the answers to most of our problems are complex, and there are no easy solutions. But until now, man has not even tried to find answers that would help the environment. Instead, decisions affecting the environment have been made on the basis of social demands, economic feasibility, or political expediency.

It is people who have demanded the products of our factories which caused pollution. It is people, encouraged by advertising, who have demanded whiter washes, fruits and vegetables unmarked by insects or blemishes, faster cars and higher octane gasolines, glossy colored papers, and throw-away bottles and cans. It is people who have demanded the products which today seriously threaten the quality of our environment.

How do social demands affect environment?

As you have already learned, in answer to the call for whiter washes, soap makers developed the first detergents, which fouled our streams and waterways, and clogged our sewage systems and home plumbing. Residents in many different areas of the nation were treated to water with a head of suds. The detergents did not break down by bacterial action. They had to be replaced with materials which did break down. The answer was the use of phosphates, readily broken down by bacterial action, and still giving a whiter than white wash. So, phosphates were added to the already overfertilized

Advertising created a demand for phosphate and caustic detergents, which threaten our water supply.

waters of America. These waters were already choked with algae and other water plants due to the overuse of fertilizers and the dumping of untreated human wastes. When Lake Erie died from decaying algae and other waterways were threatened with the same fate, the cry went out to get rid of the phosphates. Soon phosphate-free detergents were on sale, still promising whiter washes. The new whiteners were often simple table salt, baking soda, or caustic soda. Any one of these new ingredients could soon make all waterways either too salty or too alkaline to support freshwater life.

In each case, materials were added to the environment which could result in environmental change with consequences perhaps disastrous to living things. Any scientist could tell you the effects of salt or caustic soda on water balance.

There are many other examples of social demands affecting environmental decisions. The development of high compression engines and high octane leaded gasolines was due to the demand for faster cars and higher speeds. The higher speeds in turn required faster highways. The effects of highway construction and high octane gasoline on the environment have been discussed previously.

Demands for additional power have resulted in reservoir construction in fertile valleys and beautiful gorges. Demands for recreation caused the invasion of the winter wilderness by noisy snowmobiles, destruction of sand dunes by beach buggies, and ugly facilities in

An electric car, which does not burn gasoline and produce harmful exhausts, may be the answer to a pollution-free car.

the heart of the national parks. Other examples of scientifically unsound practices which have been introduced into the environment abound.

Most environmental decisions have been made on the basis of economic feasibility. "It's too expensive," has been the excuse for not stopping the pollution of air and water. Sewage disposal plants were "too expensive." Waste disposal, other than by dumping in streams or burning, was "too expensive." Poisons to control insects and disease were used because we could not afford the losses of crops and timber, and DDT and similar pesticides were cheap and effective.

How does economics affect environment?

Any control of waste disposal or recycling was considered an unnecessary expense. Waste was a part of technology, of progress. Growth depended on it. Even today, in a world threatened with environmental crisis, the cry "too expensive" is heard from many people. We can't afford to install pollution control devices in our factories. "We can't develop a pollution free auto engine by 1975," as the Congress has decreed by law, say the auto makers.

The general attitude is to go on polluting as long as possible and let society and the environment pay the bill. When strict pollution controls were imposed on pulp mills in New York, they were closed, and operations were increased in other states where pollution regulations were not so strict. This will no longer work, however. National standards will eliminate the state-jumping to escape controls.

Most interesting is the energetic publicity campaigns carried on by the polluters. During the oil spills, oil companies displayed advertisements that talked of their concern for wildlife and marine resources. Highway gasoline signs were raised fifty feet in the air to defeat the ban on billboards in the National Highway Beautification Act.

But the people are waking up. They are demanding more than pretty words and pictures. They are demanding an end to our polluted water and air, an end to destructive forest management practices in the national forests, an end to the poison-spreading programs of the Department of Agriculture, and the predator control programs of the Fish and Wildlife Service. Fortunately the new public demands are based on scientific knowledge. The old cry of "too costly" will no longer suffice.

To politicians, the environment was chiefly a place for the U.S. Corps of Engineers to construct dams. The goal of every politician was to have a big dam and reservoir in his district, hopefully named after him. Inland cities became ports for ocean-going freighters. To do this, rivers and harbors were dredged, with the dredged materials dumped in some of the nation's finest estuaries.

How does political expediency affect environment?

When the new environmental concerns were first expressed, there was little political notice. Very few men of position read *Silent Spring* when it was written by Rachel Carson in 1962. Only a few ecologists, people who could trace the complex interrelationships between environmental problems and life on earth, realized the seriousness of the environmental crisis. Was it a fad or was it a real issue, the politicians wondered. President Kennedy seemed to sense the problems as he addressed himself to the environment on a national tour shortly before his death in 1963. To President Johnson, spurred on by his wife, natural beauty was a dominant theme and pollution and deterioration of the environment drew national attention. By the time President Nixon came into office, the state of the environment was becoming a political issue. Politicians began to vie for leadership as

DDT was used indiscriminately by many to kill insects. No one thought it would also kill birds, but it did. Because we don't think of possible environmental damage, a problem's cure is often worse than the problem itself.

sponsors of legislation to control pollution. Any remaining doubts the politicians may have had about the reality of the environmental crisis were dispelled when an offshore oil well spilled its pollution over the ocean and beaches of Santa Barbara, California in January and February of 1969.

Now, the environment has become a favorite issue for Congressional sponsorship. Environmental control legislation finds many sponsors. Each bill introduced increases the funds requested for pollution control and other environmental programs. The political game is in full swing. The alligators in Florida have been protected, the cross-Florida canal project stopped at midpoint, the Alaskan oil pipeline delayed in order to pick a safe route. Congress is demanding an end to the pollution and poverty of the American environment. It is politically expedient to be a conservationist today. Some of the esthetically appealing programs, such as wilderness preservation, which drew little support a decade ago are now popular issues.

With political support, whether actual or only expedient, the future prospects of a more beautiful and bountiful environment are good, but the task will not be easy. Our fragmented government structures and the patterns of political behavior make real progress difficult. Responsibility for the environment is dispersed through a myriad of government agencies and Congressional

Alligators, distant relatives of the prehistoric dinosaur, have a commercially valuable pelt. Recently, states such as New York have banned the importation of pelts of alligators and other endangered species.

committees, some with conflicting and competing programs. One agency pays farmers to drain their land for farm crops. Another pays the farmer to set aside crop land for wildlife. Our federal timber resources are managed by several agencies, as are range and recreation resources. Even within a single wildlife agency, one department is concerned with protecting endangered species while another is concerned with the elimination of predators by poisons and trapping. Hopefully, there will soon be a department of natural resources at the federal level to coordinate all environmental programs.

The Environment and You

As you have read through this book on the environment, you have probably thought of some things you can do to make your contribution to the future of the world environment. Though it may mean giving up a few comforts, you have probably realized that we can no longer just blame the other fellow and do nothing ourselves. The poverty, pollution, poisoning and overpopulation of the environment was caused by all of us, and can only be eliminated by all of us. The following pages suggest helpful things *you* can do right now.

There are many things that can be done

What can you and your family do as individuals?

on an individual basis that would help the environment. Here are some of them:

If there are any leaky faucets in your house, have them repaired. (A dripping faucet can waste 60 gallons of water a day.)

Turn off the faucet while you brush your teeth.

Keep a jar of water in the refrigerator so you don't have to run the tap to get cold water.

Run dishwashers and washing machines only when they are full.

When possible, take showers instead of baths. (An average shower uses 10 gallons of water; an average bath, 36 gallons.)

A leaky faucet can waste 60 gallons of water a day.

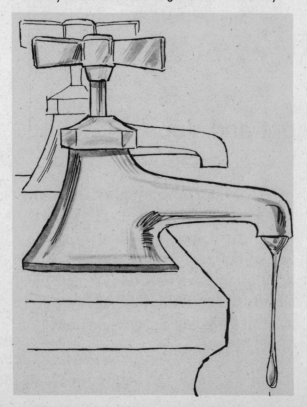

Do not use colored tissues or toilet papers which pollute the water with their dyes.

Use biodegradable, nonpolluting laundry *soap* in washing machines. If you must use a detergent, use one low in phosphates. The effects on the environment of nonphosphate detergents have not yet been proven, so their use cannot be recommended. Use low-phosphate detergent in dishwashers (it is a law in some states for manufacturers to indicate phosphate contents on detergent boxes).

Do not use the full amounts recommended on detergent boxes in dishwashers and washing machines. Keep testing reduced amounts until you determine the smallest amount necessary to do the job.

Do not use garbage disposal units. The organic material they put in drains adds to sewage treatment plant overload.

Never pour household poisons, insecticides, grease, solvents, medicines, or other chemicals down the sink drain or toilet. This will strain sewage treatment facilities. Instead, seal such items tightly and put them in the rubbish.

Do not put heavy paper, tissues, rags, disposable diapers, or other similar products into toilets. These items should be disposed of with the rubbish.

If your drinking water is obtained from a well, have it tested annually.

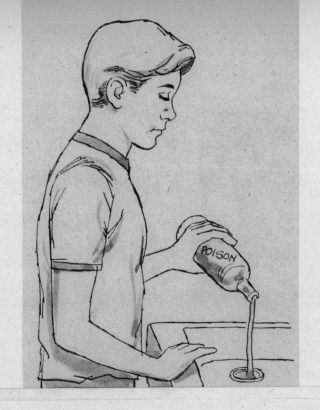

If household poisons are poured directly down the drain, they burden sewage treatment facilities.

Use paint-on oven cleaners. Sprays may cause respiratory problems.

ᔋ

Buy shampoos, lotions, mouthwashes, hair tonics and similar products in glass containers which can be recycled. (The environmental effect of burning plastic bottles is still not fully known, but is suspected to be harmful.) If you need plastic bottles in your bathroom because they are safer, buy one plastic bottle, and then refill it from glass bottles.

ᔋ

Do not burn leaves or papers. Instead make a compost heap that will enrich soil.

ᔋ

If you live in an apartment building, check to see if it has a compactor or upgraded incinerator, and if there are pollution controls on its oil burners. Report violations to local authorities.

If you have a garden, plant trees, shrubs, or berry bushes. They produce oxygen, filter dust from the air, and reduce noise. Build a birdhouse. Birds are natural enemies of insects.

Build a birdhouse in order to encourage birds on your property. They help reduce the insect population.

Green plants improve air quality by increasing oxygen in air. This is especially important in urban areas.

If you live in an apartment house, plant a rooftop garden or window box if it is not against local ordinances. Besides looking pretty, even the plants in a small window box will add to the oxygen content of the air.

Use a plow or shovel to remove snow and ice. Salt should never be used, since it can pollute water, kill trees, and irritate the paws of pet dogs and cats. Sand can be used in reasonable quantities, but it should not be used to excess. Too much sand will be washed away and clog water mains.

Use crushed stone instead of asphalt on paths and driveways. Asphalt does not allow rain to seep through and into the soil again, thus encouraging erosion.

Walk to the store or ride a bike to save use of the family car. Join an office or school car pool instead of driving an empty car; ride bikes or walk whenever feasible.

Use lead-free gasoline.

When possible, use mass transit instead of private cars.

If you drive in a city, use a small-engine car.

Keep all cars tuned, with the car's muffler, tailpipes, and pollution device, if any, in good repair.

Keep a litter bag in your car at all times, and use it. Never empty car ashtrays on the street.

Biking instead of driving helps reduce air pollution, and is also good exercise.

Don't idle your car's motor. Turn off the engine when parked or waiting.

Try to avoid using a car during rush hours. Stop-and-go traffic increases exhaust pollution.

If you live in an area that has alternate side of the street parking, obey the law. Street sweepers cannot clean streets blocked by illegally parked cars.

Do not buy products in difficult-to-dispose-of packages. Wrappings of cellophane, styrofoam, or those plastics made out of polyvinyl chloride (or PVC) give off harmful effluents if incinerated, and are not biodegradable. Mixed packaging (i.e. cardboard sides with metal tops) are hard to recycle conveniently, since components must be separated.

Do not buy individually wrapped foods. Singly wrapped cheese slices, individually wrapped bagged candies, single-serving juice cans, cans or jars wrapped together, etc. are wasteful, and also cost you, the consumer, more money.

Take a string bag or shopping bag with you when you shop, and carry purchases home in that. Refuse all excess packaging in stores.

Write to the presidents of companies that overpackage their products (especially convenience food, toy, and cosmetics' manufacturers). The com-

Don't buy overpackaged products. They waste our resources, cause pollution, and cost more to buy.

pany's name and address are usually on the label.

Use china and glass instead of paper cups and dishes.

Use cloth towels instead of paper, where possible.

Cut down on all use of paper products. Keep a blackboard for notes and messages by the phone.

Write on both sides of pads, notebook paper, and stationery.

Reuse gift wrapping. Don't overwrap presents.

Use covered refrigerator dishes instead of plastic or foil wrap.

Reuse any plastic bags, foil, or wax cardboard containers.

Save old newspapers for collection by a local environmental group.

Use returnable bottles when available. If you must use throw-away bottles or cans, take them to a recycling center when they are empty. Write to companies that bottle products in throw-away bottles or cans and tell them you will not use their products until they use returnable bottles. Visit your local supermarket and request that they stock returnable bottles, if they do not do so already. (Suppliers only provide returnable bottles to the stores at the grocer's request.)

Return extra wire hangers to your cleaner instead of throwing them away.

Do not litter. Pick up the litter you see. If you see people around you littering, tell them in a nice way that they should deposit waste in litter baskets instead of hurting the environment by throwing things on the streets.

Using a blackboard for phone messages saves paper.

Don't litter. It is unsightly, illegal, and expensive.

Curb your dog, and do not let him use the street directly in front of home or building entrances or at pedestrian crosswalks. Clean up your dog's droppings from any forbidden areas.

Bell your cat, so that birds can hear him coming.

Learn which kinds of snakes are dangerous to human beings. Never kill a harmless snake, such as a garter snake, since these animals prey on insects and rodents.

Never keep an exotic animal meant to live in the wild, such as a baby alligator or a lion cub, as a pet. Keeping such animals as pets is unfair to all concerned. The animal will be unhappy, and so will his adoptive family — since a wild animal will eventually become unmanageable and must be given away to a zoo.

Do not use DDT or other persistent poisons for insect control. Use other insecticides according to instruction and only when necessary.

If a particular type of crawling pest, such as roaches, is bothering you, use a target poison — a pesticide aimed at one type of insect — such as roach tablets.

Do not kill nonpoisonous spiders. They are the natural enemies of insect pests.

When possible, use flypaper or a fly swatter to kill flying insects, instead of aerosol or other sprays.

Do not buy things made from the furs or hides of endangered species of wildlife, such as pocketbooks made from alligator hide, coats made from jaguar or leopard fur, or cosmetic preparations made from turtle oil.

Do not purchase unnecessary electrical appliances and gadgets.

Conserve electricity during peak periods of use. Try to run major appliances such as washing machines, dryers, and dishwashers before 8 A.M., after 6 P.M., or on weekends.

When you leave a room, shut off lights, airconditioners, radio, and TV.

If possible, use approved paper and plastic garbage bags for refuse instead of heavy cans. (Approved plastic bags are not made of polyvinyl chloride, and do not cause air pollution if incinerated.) If you are still using cans, make sure lids are clamped down tightly.

In some areas, construction noise before 7 a.m. and after 6 p.m. is illegal. Report infractions to the police.

Keep TV, stereo, power mowers, and workshop tools off or at low sound level during early mornings and after 9 P.M., especially on weekends.

Don't drive with your horn. Sound the horn when safety dictates, not because you are impatient.

If large air compressors from a construction site or jackhammers on the street annoy you, protest to your local government. Devices that muffle the noise can be bought for these machines.

If you hear a bus or truck that makes an excessive noise, take the license number and send it to an official of your local government along with a letter of complaint.

Write letters to the editor of your local newspaper to encourage environmental action.

Write to companies that pollute the air or water.

Write to the elected officials who represent you — city councilmen, state assemblymen and senators, congressmen and senators — about environmental issues.

What can you do with a group? Many projects that can help save the environment can be accomplished more easily when you are a member of a group. Join the Boy Scouts, Girl Scouts, or other youth groups working for a better environment. Form an ecology club or other group. Here is a list of helpful group projects:

Ask your school administrator for a course or assembly program on the environment.

Study your community sewage system and write to officials if it is not up-to-date and efficient.

Set up a recycling center for cans, bottles, and papers if there is none in your neighborhood.

Organize a block clean-up campaign, and get everyone to pitch in to sweep up and beautify.

Look into the condition of a local park, stream, beach, or riverfront. Organize a community clean-up, paint park benches, etc.

Aluminum and tin cans, paper, and glass can be recycled. Is there a recycling center in your neighborhood?

In urban areas, join or form a smoke-watchers patrol to watch for and report incinerator violations.

❧

Set up discussion groups with local industry to find out what they are doing about pollution. (Encourage them to use glass mugs instead of paper cups at coffee breaks, install bicycle racks, donate space for recycling centers, etc.)

❧

Raise money to buy books or magazines on environmental problems and donate them to your library.

Create a park or play lot on a vacant lot.

❧

Plant trees and flowers on your street.

❧

Speak to your local supermarket manager, and encourage him to sell items in returnable bottles.

❧

Organize an ecology teach-in for your community to educate people about the dangers of pollution.

❧

Work with local officials to set up traffic lanes and paths for bicycles.

A community working together can clean up a park. Local industry will often supply trash bags, cleaning equipment, and paint and brushes for benches.

Study the traffic patterns in your town and urge that specific central streets be turned into pedestrian malls.

Study your local building construction and demolition laws. Work for the passage of laws that control amounts of airborne dust and sprayed insulating materials, particularly asbestos.

If your community does not have an anti-litter ordinance, work to pass one. If it has one, make sure it is enforced.

Study your local watershed. Is your local or state government making plans to avoid the possibility of pollution?

If your community seems too noisy, study the noise control regulations in other towns and work to pass a similar bill in your area.

Write to state and national legislators and ask them to pass bills that establish noise limits on such items as machinery and aircraft.

Are overhead utility lines and telephone poles detracting from the landscape in your area? If so, work with your town council to pass a law requiring that any new lines and cables be laid underground.

Dilapidated buildings are a health and fire hazard. Most local housing codes require their removal or improvement. If this type of building exists in your community, work with local officials for enforcement of the law.

Start an "improve the environment" contest in your area, and encourage private homeowners and local business-men to participate. Take before and after photographs of any improvements; get them published in your local newspaper, and post them in central locations.

Start a "save the trees" campaign, to prevent contractors from leveling an area prior to putting up a housing development.

Which scene would you rather look at? Working together to clean up a public eyesore helps everyone's morale.